BRITISH FREIGHT TRAINS

Moving the Goods

Paul Manley

AMBERLEY

First published 2014

Amberley Publishing
The Hill, Stroud
Gloucestershire, GL5 4EP

www.amberley-books.com

Copyright © Paul Manley, 2014

The right of Paul Manley to be identified as the Author of this work has been
asserted in accordance with the Copyrights, Designs and Patents Act 1988.

ISBN 978 1 4456 3343 5 (print)
ISBN 978 1 4456 3354 1 (ebook)

British Library Cataloguing in Publication Data.
A catalogue record for this book is available from the British Library.

Typeset in 11pt on 12pt Sabon LT Std.
Typesetting by Amberley Publishing.
Printed in the UK.

INTRODUCTION

The British freight scene has changed greatly since British Rail was privatised and the three trainload freight sectors, Mainline Freight, Loadhaul and Transrail, were sold to North & South Railways on 24 February 1996. A subsidiary of the American Wisconsin Central Railroad, North & South Railways changed its name to English, Welsh & Scottish Railway and came in to ownership of Rail Express Systems, Railfreight Distribution and National Power's freight section. Freightliner was purchased by a management buyout on 24 May 1996.

One major change is the move from mixed-wagon load traffic to more of an emphasis on block trains, with the latter being more cost-effective. The movement of coal, once the staple of rail freight in Britain, is now facing heavy changes, with the need for the UK to reduce carbon emissions. With only two deep mines left, Kellingley in North Yorkshire and Thoresby in Nottinghamshire (both owned by UK Coal), and the Scottish opencast sites shrinking, the need for imported coal has grown. In terms of tons per km, it is still the most common commodity transported by rail.

Recently introduced biomass trains have started running to Drax power station in North Yorkshire and Ironbridge power station in Shropshire. Biomass is a biological material from living or recently living organisms, and is usually carried in special, enclosed hopper wagons because it needs to be kept dry, and will be transported in pelletised form. Drax Power has invested heavily in this form of fuel, with an order of 200 specially adapted biomass rail freight wagons that will travel to the power station from the ports of Immingham, Tyne and Hull.

There has also been an increase in the supply of timber to the Kronospan works at Chirk, with trains now running from Teigngrace in Devon and Baglan Bay in South Wales to supplement the trains from Ribblehead and Carlisle Yard. The company produces various wood-based panels, decorative paper and many other supplies sold around the world.

The Jaguar Land Rover facility at Halewood, Merseyside, has seen a recent upsurge in traffic with up to three trains a day of finished cars leaving for Southampton Eastern Docks for export. The Halewood facility produces the Land Rover Freelander and the more recent success, the Range Rover Evoque, which has seen an increase in demand.

With the need to keep improving the railways and to make sure they are maintained, a few strategically situated virtual quarries/local distribution centres (LDCs) have emerged around the country. The main ones are at Carlisle, Crewe, Whitemoor, Eastleigh and Hoo Junction, with others at Doncaster, Toton, Bescot, Willesden, Westbury and Taunton. A virtual quarry/LDC is a yard where ballast is stored or stockpiled, and is supplied by block ballast trains from the various stone quarries around the country, rather than having each individual train go directly to and from the quarries themselves. The main suppliers of the stone are Mountsorrel and Stud Farm, both in Leicestershire, and Shap, in Cumbria.

Whitemoor Yard, in March, Cambridgeshire, originally served as a marshalling yard in 1929 and has also recently opened a national track materials recycling centre. The centre will deal with sleeper storage and crushing, ballast washing and decontamination and wagon maintenance among other activities, and will save thousands of tons of materials from going to landfill sites. The yard originally closed in the early 1990s and half the site is now occupied by Whitemoor Prison.

The main freight operators in Britain at the moment consist of DB Schenker, Freightliner Group, GB Railfreight, which is owned by Eurotunnel Europorte, and Direct Rail Services, owned by the Nuclear Decommissioning Authority, and Colas Rail.

The biggest British rail freight operator at the time of writing is the German company DB Schenker, which is owned by Deutsche Bahn AG. The company bought the previous biggest British rail freight operator, the English, Welsh & Scottish Railway, on 28 June 2007. They were originally going to keep the EW&S name, but on 1 January 2009 rebranded it DB Schenker. The first locomotive to receive the new DB Schenker red colour scheme was a Class 59, No. 59206, at a ceremony at the National Railway Museum in York on 21 January 2009. Their current fleet of operational locomotives and units comprises Classes 59, 60, 66, 67, 90 and 92, with the Class 325 units used for carrying mail. The company headquarters are at Doncaster, South Yorkshire.

The second-largest British rail freight operator is the Freightliner Group, owned by Railinvest Holding Company Ltd. Since being formed in 1995, it has expanded greatly from only running container trains to and from the ports around Britain. In 1999, Heavy Haul was set up and initially started running infrastructure railway trains for Network Rail, hauling ballast trains, rails and sleepers, etc., then going on to move other bulk trains including coal, cement, waste and aggregates. A new subsidiary named Freightliner Heavy Haul Ltd was set up in 2001 and these operations were transferred after initially being part of the Freightliner Group. Their current operational fleet comprises Classes 08, 66, 70 and electric locomotives Classes 86 and 90.

Direct Rail Services (DRS) started in 1995 under the ownership of British Nuclear Fuels Ltd until it was transferred to the Nuclear Decommissioning Authority on 1 April 2005. DRS commenced operating all the nuclear flask trains in Britain after taking over from the English, Welsh & Scottish Railway, and they serve destinations including Heysham, Valley, Seaton Carew and Berkeley. Also carried are the low-level waste containers, which travel a few miles down the Cumbrian coast from Sellafield to the Low Level Waste Repository at Drigg. Since then, DRS has expanded to operate many intermodal container services for several customers. The first trains started in 2002 with the Grangemouth–Daventry International Railfreight Terminal (IRT) transporting containers for both Asda and the Malcom Group, using Class 66 locomotives. Then came the Tesco Express in 2006, with these services being run for Eddie Stobart together with Tesco. These containers are carried from Daventry IRT to Mossend/Inverness, and the current traction is a Class 92 on hire from DB Schenker. Since then, many more services have started to operate. The company uses a good variety of traction that consists of Classes 20, 37, 47, 57 and 66. In January 2012, an order of fifteen Vossloh EuroLight UK locomotives was sanctioned, the first of which arrived in January 2014. They will be manufactured at the Vossloh España's factory in Valencia, Spain, and will be classed as 68s. 68002 *Intrepid* was the first locomotive to make it to the UK, and was unloaded at Southampton. Direct Rail Services headquarters are in Carlisle, Cumbria.

GB Railfreight was founded in 1999 by GB Railways before being purchased by FirstGroup in 2003 and being renamed First GBRf. Then in 2010 First GBRf was put up for sale and in June that year was bought by Eurotunnel Europorte. The company then went back to the original name with a different livery. The freight services worked by the operator include infrastructure trains, intermodal, coal and petroleum and these are hauled on the mainline by Classes 66, 73 and 92 respectively. Also part of the fleet are various shunters, two Class 08s, two Class 09s and a couple of Vanguard 0-6-0DHs that work in depots and yards. The company headquarters are currently in London.

Colas Rail was formed in 2007 and currently transports timber, steel and coal around the country. Their current operational main line fleet of locomotives consists of Classes 47, 56 and 66, with two Class 70s awaiting testing. More Class 70s have been ordered for future delivery.

I have been interested in freight trains since the early 1980s, living just a stone's throw away from the Blackburn–Hellifield line at Clitheroe, Lancashire, in the beautiful Ribble Valley. In those days the railway line was of the jointed variety and the freight trains would thunder through and certainly grab your attention! The line was reasonably busy with a variety of traction and trains; Class 40s, Class 47s and Class 25s were just a selection of the locomotives that could be observed passing through. My main station for trainspotting was Preston, because it was relatively close by and on the busy West Coast Main Line route.

As I wrote the loco numbers down, I thought it would be great to photograph them, too, and saved all my pocket money to get a little point-and-shoot camera. As I got older, I purchased a more advanced film single-lens reflex camera, and then went over to digital in around 2006.

Gradually, as locomotive-hauled passenger trains went in to a sharp decline, I started to photograph freight trains more and more. I like the challenge they bring because you never know when they are going to turn up, late, early, or not at all! My main focus was to get whatever I was photographing in full sun, but the DSLRs of today can handle most light situations very well so it is not as much of a problem.

Being born in Whalley and having lived in Clitheroe since birth, I feel very fortunate to be in this part of the world, with lots of superb locations for photographs in relatively close proximity to my home. Also, to the north is the magnificent Settle–Carlisle railway and Cumbria, and to the south-east the wonderful Peak District and Pennines. While they are not as busy as, say, the East and West Coast Main Lines, they more than make up for it with glorious scenery.

Some of my favourite photographic locations around the country include Ribblehead, Twyford Bridge just north of King's Sutton, Dunham on the Hill near Helsby, Branston south of Burton upon Trent, and Cargofleet at Middlesbrough.

Ribblehead, in North Yorkshire on the Settle–Carlisle line, has in my opinion one of the best end-of-platform shots of southbound trains in the country, using the mighty Whernside as the background. I prefer to go a little wider than the shot off the platform gives, and go out of the station down to the road, under the railway to the left and then left again up a footpath. At the top, wider views can be found, although a bit of height would be an advantage, and a pair of steps or a pole to put your camera on. With no overgrowth at the side of the line, great pictures are possible in winter, which is a rarity these days. The winter sun is good from around 11 a.m., and in summer is from around 12 p.m., with it getting off the nose just after 2 p.m. There is also a northbound shot to be had from this position, but this shot is better with the sun high, as it is a bit shadowy otherwise. For this shot, the sun is good from around 3 p.m. onwards. The majority of freight on the line consists of loaded and empty coal trains interspersed with cement, departmental, timber and gypsum workings, as required.

The shot at Twyford Bridge is on a road bridge facing south-east, and affords great views of the lovely South Northamptonshire countryside. Getting to this location could not be easier: once out of the station, just follow the footpath to your left and head north-westwards, crossing the railway at the foot crossing and heading for the road. The bridge will be to your right and there is ample room for many photographers! The best time for the northbound shot is in June because the sun gets round on the nose better. This happens after 4.45 p.m. If you plan on shooting after 7.30 p.m., I recommend bringing a decent zoom lens so as to avoid the shadow of the trees creeping into the shot. Traffic that can usually be observed here includes an empty car train, container trains and departmental workings hauled by DB Schenker, Freightliner and Colas Rail Freight respectively.

Rake Lane in Dunham on the Hill is a lovely location and the shot looking north is superb. Getting there is fairly easy, with regular buses from Helsby, although I prefer to walk from Helsby railway station, turning right at the main road and heading south-west. If going by car, there is ample parking space at the beginning of the lane. The light is probably best in June when the sun is high and is a decent angle (around 4.45 p.m. onwards) until it starts to come off the nose at around 8.30 p.m. Unfortunately, this location is not blessed with many freight trains, as most turn off at Helsby station to head to Ellesmere Port. Only the Colas Rail Freight-operated timber trains from Carlisle to Chirk are fairly regular between these times.

My next location, in Branston in East Staffordshire, is a footbridge that goes over the railway around 1 km south-west of the village on a public footpath. In between Branston Water Park and Drakelow Nature Reserve, the bridge is quite a popular location with great views of the surrounding countryside. You can also get a bit of the River Trent in your photograph. The best time of year is in June, when the sun is high and the days are long, from around 4.30 p.m. onwards (off the nose by 9 p.m.). The shot is of freight trains heading south-west, with regular coal and departmental trains operated by DB Schenker, Freightliner and GBRf. The footpath along the railway to get to the footbridge gets very overgrown, so shorts are not recommended!

The classic Cargofleet shot is off a road bridge roughly half way between Middlesbrough railway station and South Bank railway station. Facing east, the B1513 Works Road offers a great background of industrial Teesside and a view of coal, container and steel trains. The month of March before the clocks change is my favourite time of year to visit, and on a good day it can get busy around dinner time for freights heading west. The sun starts getting on the nose after 12 p.m. in winter, so you can get pictures of the dinner-time rush! Freight companies to be seen include DB Schenker, Freightliner and, at the time of writing, Colas Rail Freight, which operates a coal train to Cardiff Pengam on Saturdays, as required.

My general rule when I go to a photographic location is to always assume that the sun is going to be shining and has a nice angle, because even if it isn't you can still get a shot. If you go to a location thinking it's going to stay in, then your shot maybe backlit or on the wrong side for the sun, unless you prefer them that way of course.

One of GBRf's latest acquisitions, Class 66 No. 66748, passes Burton Salmon in charge of the 6H30 Tyne Dock–Drax Power Station loaded biomass hoppers. 18/09/2013.

GBRf Class 66 Nos 66747 and 66720 head the 6H93 Tyne Dock–Drax Power Station loaded coal hoppers and are pictured passing Copmanthorpe. The front Class 66 was on test, hence there being another Class 66 behind for insurance against failure. 29/10/2013.

GBRf liveried Class 66 No. 66745 *Modern Railways (The First 50 Years)* is photographed in charge of the 6B64 Tyne Dock–West Burton Power Station loaded coal hoppers at Sherburn-in-Elmet. 15/04/2013.

GB Railfreight liveried Class 66 No. 66744 is seen passing Colton Junction hauling the 4N36 Drax Power Station–Tyne Dock empty coal hoppers. 26/05/2012.

GB Railfreight liveried Class 66 No. 66738 passes Tommy Hall's Barn, Long Preston, with the 4B13 Newbiggin–West Burton Power Station empty gypsum containers. 19/04/2013.

Here we have GBRf liveried Class 66 No. 66742 *ABP Port of Immingham Centenary 1912–2012* accelerating through Knottingley, hauling the 4D61 Ferrybridge Power Station–Doncaster Down Decoy Yard empty coal hoppers. 24/10/2013.

Opposite page: Passing Horton in Ribblesdale, we have GBRf Class 66 No. 66727 in charge of the 4M91 West Burton Power Station–Newbiggin loaded gypsum containers on 14 May 2008.

GB Railfreight liveried Class 66 No. 66730 *Whitemoor* eases the 6H93 Tyne Dock–Drax Power Station loaded coal hoppers through Whitley Bridge. 26/05/2012.

With Ferrybridge C Power Station in the background, GBRf liveried Class 66 No. 66728 *Institution Of Railway Operators* heads the 6C09 Immingham–Eggborough Power Station loaded coal hoppers at South Moor, Knottingley, on Thursday 24 October 2013. Ferrybridge C Power Station, built in 1966, is so-called because it is the third one to be built on this site. A and B power stations were decommissioned in 1976 and 1992.

GB Railfreight liveried Class 66 No. 66727 *Andrew Scott CBE* rounds the curve at Hatton with the 6O96 Mountsorrel–Eastleigh VQ loaded ballast box wagons. 16/05/2011.

GB Railfreight Rainbow liveried Class 66 No. 66720 trundles down the slow line at Burton upon Trent with the 6V88 Beeston–Newport Docks loaded scrap on Monday 23 July 2012. The unusual livery was inspired by a girl of six and was revealed at Wansford on the Nene Valley Railway in July 2011.

Coasting through Langho we have GBRf 'Metronet' liveried Class 66 No. 66722 *Sir Edward Watkin*, in charge of the 4C52 Fiddlers Ferry Power Station–Newbiggin containerised gypsum on 18 August 2010.

GBRf liveried Class 66 No. 66718 *Gwyneth Dunwoody* is about to cross West Bank Hall level crossing on the Drax Power Station branch line with the 4N99 Drax Power Station–Tyne Dock empty biomass hoppers. 28/01/2011.

GB Railfreight liveried Class 66 No. 66715 *Valour* speeds past Whitley Bridge Junction on the 4N92 Drax Power Station–Tyne Dock empty coal hoppers. 18/02/2008.

Taking the Doncaster line at Knottingley, we have GBRf Class 66 No.
66713 *Forest City* hauling the 6F53 Tyne Dock–Cottam Power Station
loaded coal hoppers. 06/05/2008.

GB Railfreight liveried Class 66 No. 66713 *Forest City* heads the 6B72
Hull Coal Terminal–West Burton Power Station loaded coal through
Knottingley. 15/02/2013.

GB Railfreight liveried Class 66 No. 66710 *Phil Packer* keeps the 4C77 Fiddlers Ferry Power Station–Newbiggin loaded gypsum on the move. The train is photographed approaching Helsby station and is heading for Ellesmere Port to run round its train. 30/04/2013.

GBRf Class 66 No. 66711 is about to pass through Hatfield and Stainforth station with the 4R41 Eggborough Power Station–Immingham empty coal hoppers. 15/08/2008.

Opposite page: GB Railfreight liveried Class 66 No. 66710 *Phil Packer* hurries past Burton Salmon hauling the 6C13 Immingham–Eggborough Power Station loaded coal hoppers. 21/07/11.

GBRf liveried Class 66 No. 66704 *Colchester Power Signalbox* heads the 6H93 Tyne Dock–Drax Power Station loaded coal hoppers past South Moor, Kellingley. 24/10/2013.

GB Railfreight MSC liveried Class 66 No. 66709 *Sorrento* hauls the 6H93 Tyne Dock–Drax Power Station loaded coal hoppers through Knottingley, 4 October 2012. The locomotive was named and reliveried to mark the ten year partnership with the Mediterranean Shipping Company in April 2012.

GB Railfreight liveried Class 66 No. 66702 *Blue Lightning* hurries the 4L18 Barton Dock–Felixstowe intermodal service through Millmeece, near Stafford. 22/05/2012.

GB Railfreight liveried Class 66 No. 66701 slowly passes through Doncaster station in charge of the 6R46 Redcar–Immingham loaded blending coal box wagons. 24/05/2012.

Devon & Cornwall Railways liveried Class 56 No. 56312 reverberates through Sherburn-in-Elmet with the 6Z20 York Holgate Sidings–Kellingley Colliery empty coal box wagons on 4 April 2013. The locomotive is owned by British American Railway Services who, among other things, are a railway rolling stock hire company in the United Kingdom.

Cotswold Rail Class 47 No. 47828 *Joe Strummer* departs Derby after dropping off a member of crew with the 6V95 Stockton–Cardiff Tidal loaded scrap train on 4 June 2008. Cotswold Rail was a spot hire company of mainline and shunting locomotives but it dissolved in 2009. 47828 was sold to Direct Rail Services.

FASTLINE

Passing through Hatfield and Stainforth station and nearing its destination is Fastline Class 66 No. 66304 with the 4G60 Chaddesden–Hatfield Main Colliery empty coal hoppers. 15/08/2008.

Fastline Class 66 No. 66302 hurries the 4G65 Ratcliffe Power Station–Daw Mill empty coal hoppers through Tamworth on 9 September 2009. Fastline rail freight operating company was part of Jarvis Plc until they went into administration in 2010.

Fastline liveried Class 56 No. 56303 passes through the lovely Staffordshire countryside with a rather colourful 4O90 Doncaster–Thamesport container train at Elford Loop. 09/08/2007.

COLAS RAIL FREIGHT

Colas Rail Freight Class 66 No. 66849 glides past Burn, hauling the 6Z86 Wolsingham–Scunthorpe loaded coal hoppers, on 22 October 2011. The locomotive is named *Wylam Dilly* after one of the two oldest surviving railway locomotives in the world.

Colas Rail Freight Class 66 No. 66848 passes Burton Salmon in charge of the 6M86 Wolsingham–Ratcliffe Power Station loaded coal hoppers. 18/09/2013.

Colas Rail Freight Class 56 No. 56105 pounds through the Ribble Valley at Langho in charge of the 6J37 Carlisle Yard–Chirk loaded timber. Pendle Hill towers above everything in the background. 13/08/2013.

Making her way down the Blackburn to Hellifield route at Gisburn, we have Colas Rail Freight Class 56 No. 56105 with the 6Z70 Ribblehead–Chirk loaded timber wagons. 16/08/2013.

The 6E07 Washwood Heath–Boston has Colas Rail Freight Class 56 No. 56094 in charge and is pictured passing near the site of Chellaston Junction in Derbyshire. 23/07/2012.

Colas Rail Freight Class 56 No. 56094 hurries through Wigan North Western with a heavily delayed 6J37 Carlisle Yard–Chirk loaded timber train. 27/10/2012.

Helsby Hill dominates the background as Colas Rail Class 56 No. 56087 powers past Dunham on the Hill with the 6J37 Carlisle Yard–Chirk loaded timber train. 06/06/2013.

Colas Rail Class 47 Nos 47739 *Robin of Templecombe* and 47727 *Rebecca* depart Elford Loop with the 6Z48 Burton upon Trent–Dollands Moor loaded steel. 07/05/2009.

Colas Rail Freight Class 56 No. 56087 speeds through Barton, a few miles north of Preston, with the 6J37 Carlisle Yard–Chirk loaded timber train. 10/10/2013.

DRS

DRS Class 66 No. 66434 takes the back road through Warrington Bank Quay with the 4M44 Mossend–Daventry intermodal service. The loco is painted in the Malcolm Logistics livery. 02/08/2012.

DRS Class 66 No. 66433 has its turn on the 6K05 Carlisle Yard–Crewe departmental train and is passing the outskirts of Clitheroe, near Higher Standen Hey Farm. 26/08/2013.

DRS Class 66 No. 66432 rounds the curve at Gisburn with the 6K05 Carlisle Yard–Crewe. Gisburn's disused signal box can just be seen to the right of the rear of the train. 12/08/2013.

DRS have recently taken over the 6K05 Carlisle Yard–Crewe departmental train from DB Schenker and pictured in charge at Brownhill, Blackburn, is DRS Class 66 No. 66432. 16/08/2013.

The 6K05 Carlisle Yard–Crewe departmental train has now been taken over from DBS by DRS. The first day of operation saw 66428 in charge, and it is pictured at Clitheroe. 29/07/2013.

DRS Class 66 No. 66426 hurries the 4Z34 Coatbridge–Daventry intermodal through Brock. 23/05/2008.

DRS Class 66 No. 66425 speeds past Red Bank, Newton-le-Willows, on the 4S43 Daventry–Mossend Tesco Express on 1 June 2009. In the distance Fiddlers Ferry Power Station can be observed. It was commissioned in 1971 and burns both coal and biomass fuels.

DRS Class 66 No. 66426 heads the 4M44 Mossend–Daventry intermodal service at Cliff Lane, just north of Acton Bridge. 12/04/2011.

DRS Class 66 No. 66412 hurries past Winwick Junction, Warrington, on the 4M44 Mossend–Daventry intermodal. 04/04/2007.

With the failure of 66514 at Preston, DRS Class 37 No. 37610 *T. S. (Ted) Cassady* was drafted in to haul the 4S41 Fiddlers Ferry–Hunterston empty coal train and is seen here working hard through Clitheroe. 23/09/2011.

DRS Class 37 No. 37229 *Jonty Jarvis* top and tails with an unknown Class 37 hauling the 6F25 Sellafield–Runcorn empty soda/acid tanks, clagging past Warrington Bank Quay. 13/06/2006.

DRS Class 37 Nos 37194 and 37604 are pictured passing Penrith with a diverted 6K73 Sellafield–Crewe via Workington and Shap on 14 July 2011. This train had been diverted from its usual route down the Cumbrian coast because of the refurbishment of Arnside Viaduct.

DRS Class 20 Nos 20305 and 20309 on the rear work a special 6Z45 Sellafield BNFL–Crewe low level nuclear waste train and are pictured passing Red Bank, Newton-le-Willows. 04/06/2013.

DRS Class 20 Nos 20302 and 20303 head the 6M67 Bridgewater–Crewe nuclear flask train as it passes Millmeece, north of Stafford. 16/05/2012.

DB SCHENKER
AND ENGLISH, WELSH & SCOTTISH RAILWAYS

DB Schenker Class 92 No. 92034 *Kipling* hurries the 4O60 Mossend–Dollands Moor through Brock on 23 May 2008. Among the load today are some cargo wagons, with the more usual empty clay tanks at the rear.

DB Schenker Class 92 No. 92016 rushes through Warrington Bank Quay with the Fridays-only 4M63 Mossend–Hams Hall intermodal. 12/07/2013.

English, Welsh & Scottish Class 67 No. 67029 *Royal Diamond* hauls the 6G77 Burton on Trent Steel Terminal–Bescot through Burton upon Trent on 24 July 2008. This loco was painted silver in 2004 to haul the company train and in 2007 was named to celebrate Queen Elizabeth II's sixtieth wedding anniversary to Prince Philip.

DB Schenker Class 90 No. 90036 heads the 6M02 Shieldmuir–Warrington Royal Mail Terminal mail train through Wigan North Western station. This additional train ran daily for a few weeks before Christmas to help cope with the extra Christmas mail traffic. 11/12/2013.

English, Welsh & Scottish Railway Class 67 Nos 67014 and 67029 are in charge of the 6N42 Warrington Arpley–Blackburn trip working at Lostock Hall, Preston. 04/04/2007.

English, Welsh & Scottish Class 66 No. 66233 powers past Gisburn with a diverted 6S55 Burngullow–Irvine loaded china clay tanks. 02/06/2007.

English, Welsh & Scottish Class 66 No. 66232 heads the 6S00 Clitheroe–Mossend loaded cement tanks past Horton in Ribblesdale on the beautiful Settle to Carlisle railway. 15/05/2008.

DB Schenker Class 66 No. 66230 heads the 6H26 Potland Burn–Drax loaded coal hoppers at Sherburn-in-Elmet. 18/09/2013.

DB Schenker Class 66 No. 66207 heads the 6J94 Hull Docks–Rotherham empty steel wagons through Old Denaby, Mexborough. 15/03/2012.

English, Welsh & Scottish Class 66 No. 66214 departs Toton Yard with the 4T25 empty coal hoppers to Daw Mill Colliery in Warwickshire. The buildings just above the first three wagons used to be the wagon repair shop. 18/10/2007.

DB Schenker Class 66 No. 66201 heads the 6M62 Northenden–Peak Forest empty stone wagons at Ashley. 09/04/2011.

DB Schenker Class 66 No. 66197 leads the 6Z27 Hull Docks–Drax Power Station loaded biomass hoppers. 18/09/2013.

Approaching North Stafford junction is English, Welsh & Scottish Class 66 No. 66177 with a lightly loaded 4E69 Southampton–Wakefield Europort intermodal service. 04/06/2008.

DB Schenker Class 66 No. 66175 eases past Irthlingborough Road, Wellingborough, in charge of the 6E38 Colnbrook–Lindsey empty bogied tanks. 24/05/2010.

Rounding the curve at Cargofleet, Middlesbrough, is English, Welsh & Scottish Class 66 No. 66174 in charge of the 6N48 Tees Dock–Tees Yard intermodal service. 22/02/2008.

Passing North Stafford junction, Willington, Derbyshire, we have English, Welsh & Scottish Class 66 No. 66173 powering the 6E08 Wolverhampton–Doncaster covered steel wagons. 04/06/2008.

DB Schenker Class 66 No. 66170 slowly passes Common Lane, Hambleton, with the 6D72 Hull Dairycoates–Rylstone empty stone hoppers. 12/11/2013.

DB Schenker Class 66 No. 66172 *Paul Melleney* coasts down Rimington Bank on the Blackburn to Hellifield line with the 4M00 Mossend–Clitheroe empty cement tanks. 27/02/2013.

DB Schenker Class 66 No. 66168 eases the 6Z76 Newbiggin–Warrington Arpley empty gypsum containers past Barrow, near Clitheroe. 29/09/2011.

DB Schenker Class 66 No. 66161 gets the 6G45 Toton–Bescot departmental service back on the move after just having been looped and is passing Branston, Burton upon Trent. 11/07/2013.

DB Schenker Class 66 No. 66156 arrives at its destination with the 6H60 Hope Street–Peak Forest empty stone hoppers on 7 June 2011. Dove Holes Quarry dominates the background where this train will back into the sidings.

English, Welsh & Scottish Class 66 No. 66156 passes Weston, just south of Crewe Basford Hall marshalling yard, with a lightly loaded 4G63 Trafford Park–Washwood Heath intermodal service. 27/03/2008.

DB Schenker Class 66 No. 66155 speeds through Bamber Bridge with the 6Z94 Avonmouth–Clitheroe empty cement tanks. 30/07/2013.

DB Schenker Class 66 No. 66150 passes Trowell Junction with a lengthy 6M00 Humber–Kingsbury loaded bogied tanks. 04/09/2013.

English, Welsh & Scottish Railways Class 66 No. 66141 heads the 6G78 Burton steel terminal–Bescot covered steel wagons service. The train is photographed passing Kingsbury. 09/08/2007.

Rounding the curve at New Barnetby is English, Welsh & Scottish Class 66 No. 66144 heading the 6E20 Margam–Immingham steel train. 01/07/2008.

DB Schenker Class 66 No. 66126 cautiously traverses Whalley Viaduct with the 6Z35 Clitheroe–Bescot loaded cement tanks. 14/09/2013.

Above: Here we see DB Schenker Class 66 No. 66111 heading the 4M00 Mossend–Clitheroe empty cement tanks on the approach to Gisburn. Just to the right of the bodyside number, the 'Highland Stag' sticker can be observed. 13/03/2013.

Top right: DB Schenker Class 66 No. 66110 is pictured hauling the 6M96 Milford West Sidings–Tunstead empty stone hoppers at Burton Salmon, just a few miles north of Knottingley. 08/05/2012.

Bottom right: DB Schenker Class 66 No. 66110 passes Ribblehead station after just traversing over the viaduct with the 4M00 Mossend–Clitheroe empty cement tanks in tow. 16/01/2013.

DB Schenker Class 66 No. 66101 reverses into the sidings at Horrocksford Junction, Clitheroe, with the 4M00 Mossend–Clitheroe empty cement tanks on 23 January 2013. The branch line opened in 1850 to carry lime from the Old Bank Lime Works.

DB Schenker Class 66 No. 66100 heads the 6L46 Carlisle Yard–Kirkby Stephen train of loaded stone through Lancaster. 01/06/2013.

DB Schenker Class No. 66095 sweeps round the curve at Millmeece in charge of the 6M48 Southampton Eastern Docks–Halewood empty car carriers. 22/05/2012.

DB Schenker Class 66 No. 66099 passes Chellaston on the 6D44 Bescot–Toton departmental service. 03/09/2012.

English, Welsh & Scottish Class 66 No. 66092 is pictured working the 4S69 Drax Power Station–New Cumnock empty coal hoppers through Horton in Ribblesdale on 15 May 2008. Horton in Ribblesdale is a small village and civil parish in the Craven district of North Yorkshire, England, situated to the west of Pen-y-ghent.

Appearing through the mist, we have English, Welsh & Scottish Class 66 No. 66090 on a Milford Junction–Drax Power Station empty gypsum containers at Whitley Bridge. 18/2/2008.

DB Schenker Class 66 No. 66086 passes Kingsbury with the 6M85 Tyne Yard–Bescot car empties. 09/09/2009.

English, Welsh & Scottish Class 66 No. 66081 speeds through Doncaster with the 4L45 Wakefield–Felixstowe intermodal service. 02/11/2007.

DB Schenker Class 66 No. 66060 trundles through Billington on the Blackburn–Hellifield line with a Horrocksford Junction, Clitheroe, to Carlisle departmental service. 31/08/2012.

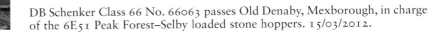
DB Schenker Class 66 No. 66063 passes Old Denaby, Mexborough, in charge of the 6E51 Peak Forest–Selby loaded stone hoppers. 15/03/2012.

Above: Trundling past Calder Bridge Junction, Wakefield, is English, Welsh & Scottish Class 66 No. 66059 with a short 6E02 Crewe–Scunthorpe departmental service. 26/03/2007.

Top right: English, Welsh & Scottish Class 66 No. 66025 heads the 6K50 Toton–Crewe departmental past Barton Turn, Barton under Needwood. 07/05/2009.

Bottom right: DB Schenker Class 66 No. 66030 passes Knottingley with the 6E84 Middleton Towers–Monk Bretton loaded sand hoppers on 7 May 2013. The sand is used for making glass at the Ardagh glass plant.

DB Schenker Class 66 No. 66020 speeds the 4M66 Southampton–Birch Coppice intermodal service through Leamington Spa. 16/05/2011.

DB Schenker Class 66 No. 66012 is pictured in charge of the 6M28 Hinksey VQ–Bescot VQ departmantal service at Twyford Bridge, near King's Sutton. 18/07/2013.

DB Schenker Class 66 No. 66010 in Euro Cargo Rail livery rounds the curve at Old Denaby, Mexborough, in charge of the 6M23 Doncaster–Mountsorrel empty ballast boxes on 15 March 2012. Euro Cargo Rail is a French rail freight operator, now a subsidiary of Deutsche Bahn.

Powering through the Peak District at Edale is DB Schenker Class 66 No. 66002 *Lafarge Quorn* with the 6M11 Washwood Heath–Peak Forest empty stone hoppers. 04/12/2013.

DB Schenker Class 66 No. 66008 is pictured at Shrivenham working a Didcot Power Station–Avonmouth empty coal hopper train. 01/11/2011.

DB Schenker Class 60 No. 60099 powers past Howsham in charge of the 6E54 Kingsbury–Humber empty tanks on 26 May 2012. This locomotive is in the Tata Steel silver livery and was painted in 2010.

DB Schenker Class 60 No. 60092 pauses for a crew change at Warrington Bank Quay station with a very late 6F74 Liverpool Bulk Terminal–Fiddlers Ferry Power Station loaded coal hoppers.16/04/2013.

DB Schenker Class 60 No. 60091 nears Mobberley with the 6H05 Oakleigh–Tunstead empty limestone hoppers. 06/08/2009.

DB Schenker Class 60 No. 60092 powers past Lostock Hall, Preston, with the 6E32 Preston Docks–Lindsey empty bitumen tanks. These new tankers replaced the old ones in November 2010 and were put together by Axiom Rail in Stoke-on-Trent. 17/05/2013.

Back in the days when Class 60s ruled the roost on iron ore trains, English, Welsh & Scottish Class 60 No. 60079 was in charge of the 6T26 Immingham–Santon loaded iron ore tipplers at Melton Ross near Barnetby. 07/07/2008.

English, Welsh & Scottish Class 60 No. 60077 propels the 6M96 Margam–Corby loaded steel past Barrow-on-Trent. 12/05/2008.

English, Welsh & Scottish Railways Class 60 No. 60076 is pictured working the 6V36 Lackenby–Margam loaded steel slabs past Elford Loop in Staffordshire. 09/08/2007.

English, Welsh & Scottish Class 60 No. 60076 powers a diverted 6E46 Kingsbury–Lindsey empty bogied tanks through Hatfield and Stainforth. 15/08/2008.

DB Schenker Class 60 No. 60074 rolls past Monks sidings, Warrington, in charge of the 6F78 Liverpool Bulk Terminal–Fiddlers Ferry Power Station empty coal hoppers. 60074 was painted in a 'powder blue' livery and named *Teenage Spirit* at the National Railway Museum in York. This was all part of a charity event for the Teenage Cancer Trust in 2008. 06/09/2012.

English, Welsh & Scottish Class 60 No. 60071 *Ribblehead Viaduct* powers the 6M04 Port Clarence–Bedworth loaded bogied tanks through Kingsbury. 09/08/2007.

DB Schenker Class 60 No. 60071 *Ribblehead Viaduct* passes Knabbs Bridge, near Melton Ross, hauling the 6V70 Lindsey to Didcot loaded aviation fuel tanks. 26/05/2012.

English, Welsh & Scottish Railways Class 60 No. 60068 *Charles Darwin* powers through Burton upon Trent in charge of the 6M82 Walsall–Tunstead empty cement tanks. 24/07/2008.

DB Schenker Class 60 No. 60065 *Jaguar* is in charge of the 6F81 Liverpool Bulk Terminal–Fiddlers Ferry Power Station loaded coal hoppers at Rainhill on 2 August 2012. The world's first inter-city railway ran through the village: the Liverpool & Manchester Railway (1830).

English, Welsh & Scottish Class 60 No 60059 *Swinden Dalesman* nears Melton Ross with the 6T24 Immingham–Santon loaded iron ore tipplers on 30 August 2007. The Kirmington Lime Works dominates the background. Loadhaul was part of British Rail's Trainload freight division when privatised and this was the colour scheme.

English, Welsh & Scottish Railway Class 60 No. 60060 *James Watt* rounds the curve at New Barnetby in charge of the 6D86 Selby–Immingham. 24/05/2007.

DB Schenker Class 60 No. 60054 powers through Clitheroe with the 6E73 Clitheroe Cement Works–Doncaster Belmont empty coal wagons. 20/09/2012.

English, Welsh & Scottish Class 60 No. 60051 heads the 6M46 Redcar–Hardendale empty lime hoppers past Cargofleet, Middlesbrough on 15 November 2007. The Lackenby steel plant can be observed in the background.

English, Welsh & Scottish Class 60 No 60046 *William Wilberforce* powers through Stourton, Leeds, with the 6M17 Leeds–Peak Forest empty stone hoppers. 07/02/2007.

English, Welsh & Scottish Class 60 No. 60048 *Eastern* heads the 6H96 Tunstead–Bredbury loaded stone hoppers between Great Rocks Junction and Peak Forest. 08/06/2006.

English, Welsh & Scottish Class 60 No. 60044 glides through Chorlton, just south of Crewe Basford Hall marshalling yard, with the 4F59 Ironbridge Power Station–Warrington Walton Yard empty coal hoppers. 22/04/2008.

English, Welsh & Scottish Class 60 No 60044 keeps the 6K22 Santon–Immingham iron ore empties on the move at Barnetby on 6 November 2007. The 'aircraft blue' and silver body stripes livery was the colour scheme of the trainload freight operator Mainline Freight, which was part of British Rail's Trainload Freight division when it was privatised.

English, Welsh & Scottish Class 60 No. 60042 *The Hundreds of Hoo* eases the 6D42 Eggborough Power Station–Lindsey empty tanks over Whitley Bridge Junction. 18/02/2008.

English, Welsh & Scottish Class 60 No. 60026 heads the 6N04 Lindsey–Jarrow loaded bogie tanks through Hatfield and Stainforth. 05/03/2008. The background is formed of Hatfield Main Colliery, which re-opened in 2007. EWS Class 66 No. 66059 awaits a path with a coal train on the right.

English, Welsh & Scottish Class 60 No. 60017 *Shotton Works Centenary Year 1996* heads the 6M55 Lindsey–Rectory Junction loaded bogie tanks past Old Denaby, Mexborough. 18/09/2008.

Gliding through Stourton, Leeds, we have English, Welsh & Scottish Class 60 No. 60020 on the 6D48 Rylstone–Dewsbury loaded stone train. 07/02/2007.

Brightening up the day, we have DB Schenker Class 60 No. 60015 powering through Clitheroe in charge of the 6L48 Farington Curve Junction–Carlisle New Yard departmental. 12/01/2014.

DB Schenker Class 60 No. 60011 heads the 6E41 Westerleigh–Lindsey empty oil tanks past Barrow on Trent. 03/09/2012.

English, Welsh & Scottish Class 60 No. 60014 *Alexander Fleming* heads the 6K23 Santon–Immingham iron ore empties past New Barnetby. 01/07/2008.

DB Schenker Class 60 No. 60010 is pictured in charge of the 6L46 Farington Curve Junction–Carlisle New Yard departmental service and is passing Clitheroe. 12/01/2014.

English, Welsh & Scottish Class 60 No. 60002 *High Peak* eases the 7F80 Liverpool Bulk Terminal–Fiddlers Ferry Power Station loaded coal merry-go-round hoppers through Warrington Bank Quay on 26 April 2007. The hoppers were called merry-go-round because a system was devised which meant the wagons could be loaded/unloaded while moving, and to avoid the need for shunting, power stations had looped tracks. Unfortunately, many collieries and pits, if any, didn't have looped tracks, so there was not officially a merry-go-round operation.

English, Welsh & Scottish Class 37 Nos 37425 *Balchder Y Cymoedd/Pride of the Valleys* and 37411 *Castell Caerffili/Caerphilly Castle* head the 6F14 Stanton Grove–Warrington Arpley at Warrington Bank Quay. 24/10/2007.

DB Schenker Class 59 No. 59202 *Vale of White Horse* is pictured at Shrivenham in charge of the 7C54 Oxford Banbury Road–Whatley empty stone box wagons. 01/11/2011.

FREIGHTLINER

Freightliner Class 90 No. 90044 heads the 4M88 Felixstowe–Crewe Basford Hall container train and is pictured sweeping through Millmeece. 22/05/2012.

Freightliner Class 90 No. 90049 speeds past Millmeece with the 4M87 Felixstowe–Trafford Park container train on 22 May 2012. 90049 is one of two Class 90s in the latest 'Powerhaul' livery, the other being 90045.

Freightliner Class 90 No. 90044 passes Tamworth Low Level station with the 4L75 Crewe Basford Hall–Felixstowe container train. 09/08/2007.

Freightliner veterans Class 86 Nos 86639 and 86605 speed past Brock with the 4M01 Coatbridge–Crewe container train on 1 June 2013. This class of locomotive is fast approaching fifty years in service after having been built in the 1965–66 period.

Freightliner Class 86 Nos 86604 and 86610 speed past Penrith hauling the 4M74 Coatbridge–Crewe Basford Hall container train on 20 May 2011. This service now sadly runs in a later path at the moment, some four and a half hours later, so photographic opportunities south of Penrith are very limited, even at the height of summer.

Freightliner Class 86 No. 86501 is pictured in charge of the 4M81 Felixstowe–Ditton container train, passing Acton Bridge on 12 April 2011. This locomotive was renumbered from 86608 in 2000 and experimentally regeared to allow it to haul trains singly.

Speeding past King's Sutton is Freightliner Class 70 No. 70016 and it is in charge of the 4O27 Garston–Southampton container train. 18/07/2013.

With the St Peter and St Paul's parish church of King's Sutton featuring prominently in the background, Freightliner's Class 70 No. 70020 sweeps through Twyford Bridge, keeping the 4M62 Southampton–Hams Hall container train on the move. 18/07/2013.

Freightliner Class 70 No. 70013 accelerates past Monks Sidings, Warrington, in charge of the 6F02 Ellesmere Port–Fiddlers Ferry Power Station loaded coal hoppers. This line is freight only and goes under Warrington Bank Quay station. 06/09/2012.

The Unilever soap factory dominates the skyline as Freightliner Class 70 No. 70010 snakes underneath Warrington Bank Quay station, hauling the 6H49 Fiddlers Ferry Power Station–Tunstead limestone empties. 17/05/2013.

Freightliner Class 70 No. 70007 approaches Acton Bridge at Cliff Lane in charge of the 4L92 Ditton–Felixstowe container train on 12 April 2011. The Class 70 locomotives were built by General Electric in Erie, Pennsylvania, and the first two arrived in the UK in 2009.

Freightliner Class 70 No. 70009 powers through Shrivenham, hauling the 4V50 Southampton–Wentloog (Cardiff) container train on 1 November 2011. Shrivenham railway station used to be located here.

Freightliner Class 70 No. 70005 rounds the curve on the approach to Helsby station with a delayed 4F03 Fiddlers Ferry–Ellesmere Port empty coal hoppers on 23 June 2011. Helsby is situated about half way between Runcorn and Chester.

Freightliner Class 70 No. 70003 heads the 6U77 Mountsorrel–Crewe VQ loaded ballast boxes near Barrow on Trent on the Sheet Stores line on 2 September 2011. This was so-called because the line from Stenson junction to Sheet Stores Junction had a factory that manufactured and repaired the tarpaulin sheets that were used to protect freight in open wagons situated close to the line near Trent Lock, Long Eaton.

Freightliner Class 70 No. 70004 *The Coal Industry Society* screams down the long straight on the approach to Sileby station with the 6L89 Tunstead–West Thurrock loaded cement tanks. 08/07/2013.

Hugging the coastline at Hest Bank is Freightliner Class 70 No. 70002, sweeping round the curve with an early running 6K27 Carlisle–Crewe departmental service. 24.06.2013.

Freightliner Class 66 No. 66951 passes Clitheroe with another load of coal for Fiddlers Ferry Power Station with the 6M11 from Hunterston. 22/08/2013.

Heading down the Ribble Valley at Gisburn is Freightliner Class 66 No. 66952 with the loaded 6M11 Killoch–Fiddlers Ferry Power Station coal hoppers. 13/03/2013.

Opposite page: Freightliner Class 66 No. 66623 *Bill Bolsover* leads the 6Z36 Blackburn–Barrow Hill loaded stone hoppers past Portsmouth on the Copy Pit line on 19 June 2012. The stone originated from Ribblehead Quarry and is taken by lorry to Blackburn.

Freightliner Class 66 No. 66951 speeds past Burton Salmon in charge of the 6R14 Immingham–Drax Power Station loaded coal hoppers on 21 July 2011. Drax is named after a nearby village and is the newest coal-fired power station in England.

Freightliner Class 66 No. 66624 passes Weston, just south of Crewe, with the 6F13 Crewe VQ–Stud Farm empty ballast box wagons. 16/06/2009.

Freightliner Class 66 No. 66621 heads the 6M96 Drax Power Station–Tunstead empty limestone hoppers through Knottingley. 07/05/2013.

Freightliner Class 66 No. 66620 heads the 6M03 Barrow Hill–Tunstead empty limestone hoppers over Great Rocks Junction in the Peak District. 17/04/2012.

Freightliner Class 66 No. 66620 heads the 6E54 Kingsbury–Humber empty bogied fuel tanks at Barrow upon Trent. 02/05/2007.

Freightliner Class 66 No. 66613 eases down Rimington Bank on the Blackburn–Hellifield route with the slightly delayed 6M11 Killoch–Fiddlers Ferry Power Station loaded coal hoppers. 27/02/2013.

Unbranded Freightliner Class 66 No. 66612 *Forth Raider* heads the 6E31 Ravenstruther–Drax Power Station loaded coal hoppers past Birkett Common. on 2 April 2009. This location is just south of Kirkby Stephen, on the Settle to Carlisle railway. The lovely Eden Valley provides part of the background.

Freightliner Class 66 No. 66608 rounds the curve at Old Denaby, Mexborough, in charge of the 6M23 Doncaster–Mountsorrel empty ballast wagons. 18/09/2008.

Freightliner Class 66 No. 66607 works the 6M91 Theale–Earles Sidings empty cement tanks at Irthlinborough Road, Wellingborough. 24/05/2010.

Freightliner Class 66 No. 66607 rounds the curve at Leamington Spa station with the 6M22 Westbury VQ–Stud Farm empty ballast boxes in tow. 16/05/2011.

Here we have Freightliner Class 66 No. 66607 heading the 6E94 Killoch–Cottam Power Station loaded coal hoppers at Colton Junction, a few miles south of York. 23/03/2010.

Powering across Whitley Bridge Junction we have Freightliner Class 66 No. 66606 with the 4S68 Eggborough Power Station–Killoch empty coal hoppers on 18 February 2008. The train is pictured coming off the branch line to/from Eggborough Power Station.

Freightliner Class 66 No. 66594 *NYK Spirit of Kyoto* passes Millmeece with the 4M61 Southampton–Trafford Park container train. 22/05/2012.

Speeding through Wellingborough at Irthlington Road, we have Freightliner Class 66 No. 66602 hauling the 6M54 Thorney Mill–Bardon Hill empty stone hoppers. 24/05/2010.

Above: Freightliner Class 66 No. 66587 makes her way through Knottingley in charge of the 4Z47 Drax Power Station–Immingham empty coal hoppers. 24/10/2013.

Top right: Being loaded at Hatfield Main Colliery in South Yorkshire, we have Freightliner Class 66 No. 66561, which will form the 6M75 to Ratcliffe Power Station. 24/01/2008.

Bottom right: On this occasion the 4D07 Wilton–Leeds container train, led by Freightliner Class 66 No. 66569, has just one container on the return working and is pictured passing Sherburn-in-Elmet, North Yorkshire. 18/09/2013.

Freightliner Class 66 No. 66557 powers through the cutting at Addingford, Horbury, with the 6E06 Bredbury–Roxby binliner on 28 June 2010. These containers carry household waste which will be dumped at the landfill site at Roxby, Scunthorpe.

Freightliner Class 66 No. 66556 passes Hatfield and Stainforth station with the 6M07 Roxby–Pendleton empty binliner. 08/10/2009.

Freightliner Class 66 No. 66552 *Maltby Raider* passes Whitley Bridge, heading the 6R33 Immingham–Drax Power Station loaded petroleum coke hoppers on 11 September 2009. The burning of petroleum coke was trialled at Drax to try and develop alternate sources of fuel. Produced from oil it contains higher levels of sulphur than ordinary coal, but by the time it gets into the atmosphere more than 90 per cent is removed.

Freightliner Class 66 No. 66549 powers an Immingham–Drax Power Station loaded coal train past Milford Junction, Monk Fryston. 21/09/2006.

Freightliner Class 66 No. 66551 awaits departure at Carlisle with the 4S07 York–Hunterston empty coal hoppers. The train has come to a halt to allow a change of crew. 03/11/2010.

Out in the wilds of Cumbria at Docker, Freightliner Class 66 No. 66546 hurries the 6Z26 Crewe Basford Hall–Carlisle departmental service. Docker is a few miles north-east of Kendal, on the West Coast Main Line.

Freightliner Class 66 No. 66544 heads the 6L16 Aldwarke–Whitemoor departmental train over Trowell Junction. 04/09/2013.

Freightliner Class 66 No. 66525 is pictured hauling the 6E73 Killoch–West Burton Power Station loaded coal hoppers through Garsdale. 14/05/2008.

Freightliner Class 66 No. 66522 speeds through Knottingley hauling the Immingham–Drax Power Station loaded petroleum coke on 8 May 2008. This locomotive was painted in the 'Shanks Waste' livery in recognition of the partnership between the two companies.

Freightliner Class 66 No. 66519 heads the 6M89 Dewsbury–Earles Sidings empty cement tanks through Horbury. 28/06/2010.

Freightliner Class 66 No. 66520 is in charge of the 4C20 Fiddlers Ferry Power Station–Carlisle New Yard empty coal hoppers past Langho. This train was one of a number diverted through here due to engineering works on the West Coast Main Line north of Preston. 25/05/2013.

Freightliner Class 66 No. 66515 coasts through Barrow, Clitheroe, on the 6Z63 Chalmerston–Fiddlers Ferry Power Station loaded coal hoppers. 13/05/2010.

Freightliner Class 66 No. 66514 eases the 6M07 Roxby–Pendleton empty binliner through Agbrigg, Wakefield. 23/06/2008.

Freightliner Class 66 No. 66511 heads the 6D45 Luton–Mountsorrel empty self-discharge stone train through Sileby on 24 August 2010. The self-discharge trains are a set of wagons that have a conveyor belt underneath them with an unloading vehicle at one end, negating the need for specialised unloading equipment.

Freightliner Class 66 No. 66513 is about to cross West Bank House level crossing with a Drax Power Station–Kelingley Colliery empty coal hoppers. The level crossing is situated on the Drax branch line. 28/01/2011.

Freightliner Class 66 No. 66511 heads the 6M23 Doncaster–Mountsorrel empty ballast box wagons through Hasland, Chesterfield. 10/06/2008.

In some pretty amazing light, Freightliner Class 66 No. 66509 heads the 6Z87 Ravenstruther–Ratcliffe Power Station loaded coal hoppers on 19 February 2008. Blea Moor is in the beautiful Yorkshire Dales National Park.

Freightliner Class 66 No. 66508 is dwarfed by the might of Whernside as it keeps the 6M11 Killoch–Fiddlers Ferry Power Station loaded coal hoppers on the move at Ribblehead. 02/03/2011.

Freightliner Class 66 No. 66508 passes Cossington, north of Leicester, in charge of the 6L45 Earles–West Thurrock loaded cement tanks. 19/05/2011.

After just leaving the East Coast Main Line at Hambleton South Junction, Freightliner Class 66 No. 66506 *Crewe Regeneration* heads the 6R10 Immingham–Drax Power Station loaded coal hoppers. The location is Common Lane, Hambleton. 12/11/2013.

Freightliner Class 66 No. 66504 heads the 4M94 Felixstowe–Ditton container train through Acton Bridge in Cheshire. 27/04/2006.

Freightliner Class 66 No. 66501 *Japan 2001* heads a lightly loaded 4O54 Leeds–Southampton container train through Kingsbury on 9 August 2007. The line off to the right near the back of the train goes to the oil terminal, and the scrap trains are loaded here.

On hire to Freightliner, we have Direct Rail Services Class 66 No. 66425 passing Barrow on Trent with the 6M49 Barrow Hill–Rugeley Power Station loaded coal hoppers. 12/05/2008.

Freightliner Class 57 No. 57002 *Freightliner Pheonix* snakes round the curves at Whitacre Junction, hauling the 4L93 Lawley St–Felixstowe on 7 September 2006. These particular class of locomotives are also known as 'Bodysnatchers' because the body was originally a Class 47 that has been modified.